PIT BULLS

Vintage photographs of Pit Bulls and the people who loved them

Anthony M Julian

Pit Bulls: Vintage Photographs of Pit Bulls and the People Who Loved Them

FIRST SUNBURY PRESS EDITION
Printed in the United States of America
April 2013

ISBN 978-1-62006-211-1

Published by:
Sunbury Press, Inc.
50-A W Main St
Mechanicsburg, PA   17055

www.sunburypress.com

INTRODUCTION

While researching and obtaining old photographs for this book, one thing was evident; the pride and admiration past owners had for their Pit Bulls. Most of America was rural and our nation was still growing. Life was hard, family was first, and the working man took pride in what he had. There were no leash laws or importance placed on a particular breed. It was just your dog.

Breed-specific legislation didn't exist, and there was no media frenzy to fuel myths and unjust hatred about the Pit Bull. And why not? The Pit Bull was a symbol of our nation's courage and determination, and held a place in our history as decorated war heroes, loved family pets of actors, presidents, socialites, famous military generals, and an adored companion to a bunch of "Little Rascals". Long forgotten, during the Civil War, a Pit Bull even stood watch over our dead solders for three days until help arrived.

In those days, over-breeding and bad genetics were non-existent and people appreciated the history of the Pit Bull. It was a working dog that the owners were proud to have; so much so that they were included in the family photo, a big and costly event back in the day. The Pit Bull was the most popular dog in America and we loved it for what it was and wasn't. It was and still is the most versatile dog in our history.

We can't ignore what the Pit Bull was bred for. This is the breed's history and to try and take it away from them wouldn't be fair. But, we also need to remember the breed's loyalty for us then and now. We owe them at least that much.

So, sit back, grab a cup of joe, and enjoy some pretty amazing photographs of pit bulls, pit-mixes, and the people who loved them.

This book is dedicated to Max
our adopted Lab/Pit mix who showed us how special these dogs
truly are. His love, loyalty, and comic ways have taught us that
second chances come when you least expect it. Without him this
book may have never been a reality.

And to all the Pit Bulls
in these amazing photos, those past and present, I thank you for
showing me the truth. With understanding, education, and
respect, perhaps we'll someday ask that you forgive us for our
ignorance and give you once again your rightful place in our
nation's history and our hearts.

DISCOVERY

If someone would have told me ten years ago that some day I'd be doing a book of early candid photos depicting Pit Bulls as cherished family pets, I would have said they were crazy. Up until that point, I had only heard bad media reports of this breed and horror stories of how these dogs were aggressive and lived for nothing more than to attack people.

After I began volunteering at a local canine rescue, I realized that all of the horror stories I had heard couldn't have been any farther from the truth. Not only did I find Pit Bulls to be some of the best dogs in the shelter, but my wife and I eventually adopted one from there—a five-year-old Lab/Pit mix named Max who is an absolute sweetheart.

I eventually started researching Pit Bulls and volunteering my time with a local organization that promotes public awareness—educating the public and teaching responsible ownership of this breed. I soon learned the breed were not the monsters I had heard about, but, in fact, one of the most intelligent, loving, social, comical, athletic, and determined dogs I have ever known.

Pit Bulls crave human contact, so much so, that their puppies prefer our company to their mother's two weeks before all other dogs. They are also wonderful with children. In temperance tests of all breeds, the most tolerant was the Golden Retriever. The second most tolerant was the Pit Bull. It seemed there were more positive attributes about this breed than all of the negatives I was always told about. Max certainly proved this to be true, as did my research into the history of the Pit Bull.

So, what happened along the way to make our society regard what was once honored as a WWI hero, known as AMERICA'S dog and cherished as a family companion, into a monster that the media has so negatively portrayed at every opportunity?

Abused, abandoned and banned in many cities throughout the country, Pit Bulls, more than any other breed in our nation's history, over-fill more shelters than anyone can imagine. My research has made it clear to me there is a need for a book showing the love we, as a nation, had at one time for these dogs. Through candid vintage photos, not just studio portraits, we see people interacting with their Pit Bulls and Pit mixes. They obviously loved these dogs and from these photos, it is apparent they were valued members of the family. Given that, in those days, having a picture taken was a special occasion indeed, it is even more endearing that they wanted it taken with their beloved Pit Bull.

It is not my intent to go into great detail about the facts and history of the Pit Bull. There are plenty of websites and books dedicated to just that. Instead, I will share interesting facts revealing just how much the Pit Bull has been ingrained in our nation's history—more so than any other dog.

WHAT'S IN A NAME

The name Pit Bull is a term comprising three distinct breeds: The American Pit Bull Terrier, American Staffordshire Terrier, and Staffordshire Bull Terrier. Originating in England and Ireland, their history goes back much farther than in the United States. Originally they were known as Bulldogs, not what we consider Bulldogs of today, but dogs bred for actual bull-baiting.

Bull-baiting is believed to go all the way back to the time of the Romans. It eventually became a way for the lower classes to take out aggression and frustration. By the 1700s, Bulldogs, such as the Scottish Blue Poll and the Irish Alunt, were commonly forced to go in the ring and bite bulls on the ears. The pretense was that being bitten by the dogs would actually tenderize the meat of the bull. In reality, it was an urban legend to help perpetuate the tradition so that gamblers could profit. In 1835, the British public took a stand and was able to have Parliament finally ban the cruel act of bull-baiting. Unfortunately, many Bulldog breeders still saw the potential for the breed to be profitable as fighters. This was when they started breeding a new type of dog, which they called the Staffordshire Bull Terrier. The breed was much more agile and fine-tuned enabling it to earn quite a reputation as a dog-fighter.

Up until the events in 1835, there was no "pit" in Pit Bull. This evolved from the act of ratting, where Bulldogs were dropped into pits full of rats for a fixed duration. People would then speculate about how many rats would be killed. It was the rat pit that turned the Bull and Terrier into the Pit Bull Terrier. This harsh reality, Pit Bulls, with their strong Terrier instincts, tremendous strength, determined prey drive, and their history as fighting dogs, made them what they are. They were never bred for human aggression but they can be dog-aggressive. It's their heritage and history we can't ignore.

COMING TO AMERICA

It was in the early 1800s when Bull and Terriers were first transported to the United States and Canada with various immigrants. It wasn't until 1898 that the breed was actually recognized as the American Pit Bull Terrier.

When English and Irish immigrants came to America, they brought, along, with their beloved Pits, the cruel act of dog fighting. Wicked in every sense of the word, some aspects of dog fighting were different than today. For instance, owners would take each other's dogs and give them baths before the fight. When a dog was injured, someone would tend to the wounds. Pit Bulls were chosen because of their strength, agility, good temperament with their handlers, and their desire to please their owner, even if it meant fighting to the death.

However, the majority of Pit Bulls, during that era, were working dogs that helped on farms, were great hunting companions and were the family dog of choice. This was as true in England and Ireland as it was in America.

Amazingly, Pit Bulls were preferred family companions and favored by many as an excellent all-around dog. They accompanied westward-bound pioneers as they traversed the wilderness.

A PLACE IN HISTORY

One of the most famous Pit Bulls of all time was Petey from "The Little Rascals." Petey was, in fact, an American Pit Bull Terrier. He was the first Pit Bull to be dual registered as an American Pit Bull Terrier and Staffordshire Terrier. If you were to ask anyone at the time about "Our Gang" or "The Little Rascals," they would all remember lovable Petey.

The great silent film comedian Fatty Arbuckle owned a Pit Bull named Luke, who was featured in many of his films. In 1903, the first coast-to-coast trip in an automobile was made by H. Nelson Jackson (physician and businessman) and his trusty companion, a Pit Bull named Bud the Dog. Dr. Jackson even had goggles made for Bud. These are now on display at the Smithsonian Institute.

The most decorated war dog of WWI was Stubby a Pit/Terrier mix. He endured 17 battles, was promoted to sergeant, met President Woodrow Wilson, went to the White House twice and met Presidents Harding and Coolidge. He was awarded the medal for heroism by The Humane Society of the United States and General John Pershing, Commanding General of the United States Armies. After Army duty Stubby became the official mascot for Georgetown University and made many public appearances in parades.

During the Civil War, the mascot for the 11th Pennsylvania Volunteer Infantry Regiment was Sallie, a Bull Terrier who not only fought alongside her regiment in many battles, but was acknowledged in a parade by President Abraham Lincoln. Sallie was killed at the battle of Hatcher's Run. Through fierce gunfire, the men of the 11th Regiment tearfully buried her body on the spot she was found dead. She's immortalized in bronze at the foot of the 11th Regiment monument in Gettysburg.

Other notable Pit Bulls were Nipper, the company mascot for RCA Victor (though some say he was a fox terrier), and Tige, the lovable companion of Buster Brown of Buster Brown shoes. Pit Bulls were used on the cover of Life magazine three times—more times than any other breed.

Famous people who have owned Pit Bulls are many, including President Theodore Roosevelt, President Woodrow Wilson, General Patton, Helen Keller, Thomas Edison, Fred Astaire, John Steinbeck, Humphrey Bogart, Rachel Ray, Linda Blair, Michael J. Fox, Jessica Biel, Cesar Milan, Madonna, Alicia Silverstone, Anthony Robbins, and the list goes on and on.

So what happened to this popular breed of dog that was once the most popular in America—as celebrities, war heroes, mascots for many college football teams of the era, cherished family pets of working men and the rich, and symbols of strength for our country?

Thanks to the media frenzy surrounding every negative incident and the exploitation of the breed by drug dealers and inner city thugs, the Pit Bull has been caught in the middle of unjust hatred fueled by myths, and an uneducated public.

Additionally, they are over-bred by backyard breeders, resulting in unstable temperaments and poor genetics. All too often, they have been the victims of horrible acts of cruelty and neglect. They've been abandoned on the streets and tossed onto highways.

Have we, as a society, turned our backs on one of the most loyal and versatile dogs this country has ever known?

Perhaps the tide is finally turning.

HOPE FOR THE FUTURE

Rescue groups, Pit Bull organizations, and people in general, are starting to spread the word of the positive side of this great breed by holding fundraisers, weight pulling and agility competitions, and adoption days with emphasis on the breed's positive qualities and true nature.

At one of the local vaccination clinics for dogs and cats, I noticed Bad Press, a local organization that helps spread the positive image of the breed. At their stand, I found old-time photos of people and their Pit Bulls that got me thinking. Why hasn't anybody done a book about days gone by with candid photos of Pit Bulls, Pit mixes, and the people who loved them--not just studio photos, but also real candid photos of the interaction of the owners and their Pit Bulls in everyday situations?

After deciding to do this book, I began by searching the Internet for historic and vintage photos. What I found amazed me. Here were real photos of people and dogs interacting. And, judging by the photos, the feeling of love and admiration between owner and dog was mutual. Here were photos of Pits with young girls and boys, beautiful women, proud men, stern men, hard-working common folk, well-dressed folk, babies and cats. These dogs were proudly included in the family photo, sitting on a chair, and riding in fancy old cars—hugged by men, women, and children, who obviously loved these dogs.

All of the negativity I had heard about this breed over the years suddenly washed away as the truth came to light. These were dogs that people loved and respected and they were a part of the family. People were proud of their Pit Bulls and it showed on their faces.

These weren't the monsters that we were lead to believe, but actual FAMILY pets. They were hard workers for the common man, best friend for the children, and proud dogs of the rich. They were used as police dogs, therapy dogs, and in rescue work. They were celebrated on postcards, greeting cards, and WWI propaganda posters, symbolizing strength, courage, and determination of our country.

"Pit Bulls" was chosen as the title of this book for all the Pits that came before and will come after. Let us not forget or forsake this wonderful breed. It has stood beside us for hundreds of years and ingrained itself into our history. And, despite everything it has experienced, it never once turned its back on us.

-- Anthony M. Julian

Popular with the working class, the Pit Bull was the dog of choice.
Strong, loyal, and determined.

Circa: early 1900s

Studio portrait of two well-dressed gents with their Pit Bull.

Circa: 1918

During the early years of the 20th century, dogs often
accompanied Navy and luxury liners, as mascots.
Among more popular were Pit Bulls.

Circa: 1913

Two lovely women in beautiful white dresses
and a young boy with his best pal, his Pit Bull.

Circa: 1920s

Mother and daughter standing proudly next to their new car
and family pet, their Pit Bull.

Circa: 1914

Cute girl with her faithful guardian, her Pit Bull.

Circa: 1930s

A special occasion indeed. The family portrait with their nursing female Pit Bull. Nosy neighbor peering through her window (right)

Circa: early 1900

Early cabinet photo of working class man with his two pals.

Circa: early 1900s

Fancy studio portrait of a "well to do" man with his very
proud and attentive Pit Bull.

Circa: early 1900s

Studio portrait of an adorable little boy and his best buddy,
a small Pit Bull with a bow.

Circa: late 1800s

Young child with their loyal and protective Pit Bull

Circa: early 1900s

Studio photo of a young boy wearing a "Little Lord Fauntleroy" suit, along beside his attentive and playful Pit Bull.

Circa: appx. 1885

Family gathering in their Sunday's best for a group photo.
Including their beloved Pit Bull.

Circa: late 1800s

Early rural life. Eva Ashlock and friend, along with a neighbor girl. And of course the ever present guardian, the Pit Bull.

Circa: late 1800s

Cigarette Card: actress Thelma Todd
(aka: Ms. Crabtree and Petey) from "Our Gang"

Circa: 1930s

Early Picture Postcard.
Beautiful well-to-do lady with her Staffordshire Bull Terrier.

Circa: 1907

Not only were Pit Bulls valued family pets, they were loved and adored. The feeling was mutual.

Circa: 1918

Best Friends

Circa: 1920s

A great way to spend the afternoon

It was a time before fancy dog groomers. All you needed was a
river and some soap

Circa: Pre 1920

Mom, baby and proud Pit Bull

Two young boys out for a ride in their buggy with their best
buddy, their Pit Bull

Circa: late 1860s

Early life on the farm. Proud dad, baby and, of course, the Pit Bull.

Pit Bulls and the working man went hand in hand. No wonder they were America's favorite breed. Jim DeVaney and Buster.

Circa: 1918

Elwood, Freshman at OU, with Star car and Buddy Boy.

Circa: 1934

Early farm life photo with the trusty family Pit Bull. On the back of photo is written "Martha is still eating"

Circa: 1930s

Best buddies

Estate photo

Circa: 1920s

Dressed in Sunday best, two brothers pose
for a photo with their Pit Bull.

This photo was one of many from an estate sale that showed this lady with her beloved Pit Bull from the time it was a puppy and throughout it's life.

Circa: 1920s

Lov'in on his Pit Bull

A well-to-do gentleman with his Pit Bull.

Circa: 1918

Family portraits

Circa: 1930

Buster the Pit Bull.

California, circa: 1918

A girl's best friend.

Verna and her Pit Bull.

Oregon, circa: 1913

After "Little Rascals", Petey retired to Atlantic city's Steel Pier
where he would pose with thousands of admirers.

Circa: 1930s

The Pit Bull and the lady.

Cute girl with her pal, a Pit mix, sitting on his own cat chair.

Circa: 1918

For many during the early part of the 20th century, life was hard. Yet there's a gentleness in her expression and how she holds her Pit Bull puppy. Back of photo reads: Mrs. Ida Donley born July 19, 1870

Cabinet photo: Adorable boy in his "Little Lord Flaunteroy" outfit with his attentive Pit Bull buddy.

Minnesota, circa: 1880s

Brother and sister with their Pit Bull. Love the boy's hat.

Circa: 1930s

Lady with her faithful
Staffordshire Bull Terrier.

Early cabinet photo of young boy with his Pit
Bull holding a bucket.

Circa: 1880s

Great cabinet photo of a boy taking his Pit
Bull for a ride in his pedal car.

Circa: 1913

Cabinet photo of an adorable little girl and
her protective Pit Bull Terrier.

Circa: 1800s
(cover)

Cabinet photo of a man and wife and their inquisitive Pit Bull.

Circa: late 1800s

Cabinet photo of a man and wife and their
Pit Bull.

Rochester, New York, circa: late 1800s

Mother and daughter taking their Pit Bull for a drive.

Circa: 1914

Buddies for sure.

Cute girl playing in a wicker basket as your loyal Pit Bull
watches over her.

Circa: 1900s

Photo taken from a glass negative. Two pretty girls holding their beloved Pit Bull.

Circa: 1915

Grandma and grandchild with one happy Pit Bull.
Back of photo reads: Dodge 1920.

Circa: 1920

Cabinet photo of two girls with two white Pit Bulls. Photo reads
"Hanna adopted by Aunt Carrie, Mother Augusta Sawyer"

Circa: 1918

Early photo of football team and their Pit Bull mascot. Pit Bulls were mascots for many teams back during the turn of the century.

Circa: 1906

Well-dressed lady with her Pit Bull.

Circa: early 1900s

Postcard portrait of lady with her Staffordshire Terrier.

Circa: 1915

Smiling lady with her Pit Bull buddy.

Circa: 1920s

A well-dressed man, with his trusted Pit
Bull.

Two friends with their Pit Bull
taking center stage.

Real photo postcard entitled "Lucky Dog."

Circa: 1908

Early rural photo of grandma in her bonnet (or night cap),
with the grandkids and their watchful Pit Bull

Oregon, circa: 1913

ACKNOWLEDGMENTS

It is with the utmost appreciation and gratitude that I want to thank the following individuals for helping me to make my dream a reality. Without their support and inspiration none of this would have been possible:

To my wonderful wife who believed in my vision and was understanding every time new pictures arrived in the mail. Thank you for your unwavering strength, devotion, and love you've shown me through all these years. To all the sellers on the Internet of these great vintage photos who opened my eyes to a part of history I never realized was there. Especially to Deanna Hamilton who sold me the most amazing photos and along the way became a great friend. To all the volunteers at the Canine Rescue of Central PA who gave me the wonderful opportunity of helping with all of the shelter dogs. This was the trigger that would start me on this journey and bring me to this point. To Lori Zimmer of Bad Press and Dr. Mimnaugh (DVM) for their expertise and sharing their valued time to look at the photos for the book and confirming all of the dogs as being true Pits and Pit mixes.

Last but not least to our dog Max, our adopted Lab/Pit mix who showed us how amazing these dogs really are. He has shown us the love, loyalty, and how fun these dogs are. Without him, this book may never have been done.

RESOURCES

Mann,J.(n.d.)Fighting Pit Bull-Dog Fighting and the American Pit Bull Terrier. Retrieved from www.pitbulllovers.com/fighting-pit-bull-dog-fighting.html

Grossman,Y.W.(May 4,2011. FOR OVER ONE HUNDRED YEARS AMERICANS KNEW PIT BULLS FOR WHAT THEY DID BEST. BABYSITTING. PART I. Retrieved from http://www.ywgrossman.com/photoblog/?p=676

Amymarie 5.(n.d.)Facts about Pitt Bulls 87. Retrieved from http://amymarie5.hubpages.com/hub/Facts-About-Pit-Bulls

Pitbull Training 101.(n.d.). Retrieved from www.pitbulltraining101.com/american-pitbull-terriers-history/

Pitbull Advocate 101.(n.d.). Retrieved from www.pitbulladvocate101.com/owns.php

Boldog Training Kennel Informational Site. (n.d.).Retrieved from www.workingpitbull.com/aboutpits2.htm

The Pit Stop Santuary. (n.d.) Retrieved from www.thepitstopsanctuar.com/historyofthepitbull.htm

Sallie, Mascot of the 11th PA VOL. Infantry. (n.d.). Retrieved from http://www.nycivilwar.us/sallie.html

Made in the USA
San Bernardino, CA
14 December 2016